T0065523

GOD'S HEALING ENVIRONMENT

Living the Christian Life
While Going through Challenges

EDWARD HARRIS SR.

WESTBOW
PRESS®
A DIVISION OF THOMAS NELSON
& ZONDERVAN

WestBow Press books may be ordered through booksellers or by contacting:

WestBow Press
A Division of Thomas Nelson & Zondervan
1663 Liberty Drive
Bloomington, IN 47403
www.westbowpress.com
844-714-3454

Unless otherwise noted, scripture taken from the King James Version of the Bible.

Scripture marked (NKJV) taken from the New King James Version®. Copyright © 1982 by Thomas Nelson. Used by permission. All rights reserved.

ISBN: 978-1-6642-0204-7 (sc)
ISBN: 978-1-6642-0205-4 (e)

Print information available on the last page.

WestBow Press rev. date: 09/10/2020

To my wife, Sheli,
For her love and support during a very difficult
season for me at the death of my mother.
And also to all who would receive their healings from the Lord.

CONTENTS

INTRODUCTION

In the Healing Environment

When I think about everything I have been through in my personal life, I have to thank God for reminding me that I was a man on a mission. Through all my challenges and difficulties, God helped me to move into a place of healing, which was found only in Him. I used to hear other Christians call Him a deliverer, a healer, and a restorer, but it wasn't until my mother went home to be with the Lord that I realized for myself that God is able to heal all pain and heartache. The hurt that was in my heart after losing my mother was so painful. In my most challenging time, I found my healing environment in God's Word. His Word provided me a place where I could go and not be judged as a man, as a pastor, or as a Christian. The Bible teaches us that God sent not His Son into the world to condemn the world in John 3:17 (NKJV). We must never forget that the world, through Jesus Christ, was saved by God's grace. The person who believes in Him is not condemned, but anyone who does not believe is condemned already. I learned in this healing environment that even when I felt depressed, and many times I did, in Christ I was free from the bondage of my pain and depression. The less I focused on me and what I was going through and began to really trust God at His Word, the more peace I felt as I went through my challenging season. We have to know that "He hath borne our grief and carried our sorrows. yet we did esteem Him stricken, smitten of God, and afflicted. Jesus was wounded for our transgressions, He was bruised for our iniquities; the chastisement of our peace was upon Him and by His stripes we are healed (Isaiah 53:4–5

NKJV). As Christians, we have to understand that if we are going to survive the difficult experiences in life, we must trust in the Lord to direct our paths. We have to learn how to trust in the power of God because He will make a way for us in every situation life brings our way. We also have to stand strong on the promises of God.

Numbers 14:2 (NKJV) teaches us that in the midst of the difficulties of life, you can still bring glory to God in how you handle life challenges. God wants us to know that He has covered all the bases, and He is the One who is in total control of producing the outcome. We need to know that the reasons we go through difficulties are because God loves us and is using situations to draw us closer to His perfect will for our lives. Stand strong in your time of challenge because those experiences are necessary for us to see that the will of God for our lives is greater than our feelings, our pains, our heartaches, and even our personal ambitions. Ephesians 6:11 (NKJV) says that we should put on the whole armor of God that we may be able to stand against the wiles of the devil.

We are on a mission from God. We are not just here to survive through the challenges of life. We are here to thrive and grow in God's grace and knowledge while we go through life's challenges. Jesus declared that it was finished, and the phrase, "It is Finished" (John 19:30), takes on the meaning of completing the task or the agenda that God the Father set in motion. His plan and purpose are still in progress, and God wants us to know that He will never fail us or push us beyond what we are able to bear. As we continue to trust in God's healing environment, we will be able to see God's will for our lives through our faith in the Lord. Remember that God does not change; whatever He promises in His Word will happen. God has everything under control. I have learned that it is not God's will that we be pushed around and beaten down by our problems in life. I am grateful today because of God's healing environment and that I found strength not to give up. I want to encourage you to trust in God for everything you need. He will see you through those dark places in life. God bless you!

CHAPTER 1

❧

I Am Ready for Change

Whoever offers praise glorifies Me; And
to him who orders his conduct aright I
will show the salvation of God."
—Psalm 50:23 (NKJV)

Joshua was Moses' successor and led the Israelites into the Promised Land.
Regardless of whether Joshua fully understood the destination of God's
plan for his life, God set his life on course. Joshua's life was predestined for
great things. Predestination is God's way of telling us that everything in
our lives has already been worked out for His greater good. The realities
of our personal relationships with God through Jesus are that we are being
divinely set up to be spiritually blessed. The Bible tells us in Ephesians 1:11
(NKJV) that we have obtained an inheritance, and we have been predestined
according to the purpose of Hewho worked all things after the counsel of
His own will. There are many analogies that may help us understand this
doctrine of predestination: (a) the plan of God is like the architect's plan,
drawn first in his mind and then on paper according to his intentions and
design; (b) God's plan may be like being a basketball coach who has carefully
conceived a game plan his team seeks to carry out; and (c) He is like the
student who plans his semester schedule very carefully so that he is able to
do well on all required assignments.

We must understand that God determines beforehand our final goal

1

and guarantees that we will meet the objective. Romans 8:30 (NKJV) tells us that whom God did predestine, He also called. "Pre" refers to the idea of time, or before our life-journeys ever began. "Destination" refers to goal for which our lives move. Romans 8:28 (NKJV) teaches us that all things work together for good to those who love God and are called according to His purpose. We must understand that God's power is in front of our problems. He is the authority of our directions. Predestination is a very hopeful and encouraging truth. We must understand that it is God who predestined our lives and gives us a deep confidence in His eternal security. It is not our responsibilities to figure out our lives. It is God who will fully accomplish His plan for each of us.

CHAPTER 2

❧

The Wilderness Can Help You

> Surely He hath borne our griefs
> and carried our sorrows;
> yet we did esteem Him stricken,
> smitten of God, and afflicted.
> But he was wounded for our transgressions,
> He was bruised for our iniquities:
> the chastisement of our peace was upon
> Him; and by His stripes we are healed.
> —Isaiah 53:4–5 (KJV)

We are living in a world where we don't have to be suicidal to wonder if our lives are worth living. We don't have to be locked behind bars to feel like we are imprisoned. We don't have to be on skid row to feel like we are losers. We don't have to be psychotic to run from the deeper issues of life. We don't have to get beaten up by a heavyweight fighter to feel like we have been defeated. We don't have to be a millionaire to feel as if we are selling out to material wealth. Most people have an urgency not to look like a person who is struggling and going through trials and tribulations.

As Christians, we must understand three things that are essential if we are going to thrive in the wilderness experience. First, we have to trust in the Lord for our directions in life. We must learn to trust in the power of God because He will make a way for us, no matter what life might bring our way.

Second, we must stand strong on God's promise. Numbers 14:2 (NKJV) teaches us that in the midst of the situation or circumstance, God wants to be glorified. God wants us to know that He has covered all the bases. We need to learn to stand strong because these experiences are necessary in order for us to see that the will of God for our lives is greater than just being ambitious. In Ephesians 6:11 (NKJV), the Bible says that we should put on the whole armor of God that ye may be able to stand against the wiles of the devil. Third, commit to God's way. In other words, do not rely on your plans, your degree, your bank account, your friends, your relatives, your job, or your intellect because these things may fail you. The Bible says in Psalm 37:5 (KJV), "Commit thy way unto the Lord, and trust also in him, and he will bring it to pass." God wants to bless us, and we can either go back to doing what we used to do, or we can move into God's promise for our lives.

CHAPTER 3

─────────── ✦ ───────────

He Will Do It

If you abide in Me,
and My words abide in you, you shall ask what you will,
and it shall be done unto you.
—John 15:7 (NKJV)

Life can sometimes present us with many burdens to bear. The trials and tribulations of life can be overwhelming. Something in our lives can cause us to laugh today and cry tomorrow. We can be happy today and sad tomorrow. One day we can be on top of the world; everything is going right. The next day we can be hit with bad news that can bring us down in the dumps. One day we can have everything in order, and the next day, our lives can be falling apart. As believers, we're not immune to trouble. Yet sometimes in our daily experiences, we can go from high mountain moments to low valley challenges. When we are in the valley, God is still there, working that situation out for His glory. The Bible teaches us in Psalm 56:11 (NKJV) that we should trust God and not be afraid of what man might do to us.

Daniel was taken into captivity before the fall of Jerusalem. Daniel had the gift of prophesy and the interpretation of dreams. Daniel was given a position of authority over the Babylonian scientists, but he lost that position because of charges brought against him by the government. Daniel was later restored to the position of prominence because he put his trust in God's will. Daniel was obviously an intelligent and righteous man, trusted even by worldly people and pagans in high positions. But he was not immune to trouble; he was thrown into a lion's den. We must understand that the lions were there to cause fear and doubt; lions could represent the devil and his principalities. The scriptures teach us that the devil is like a roaring lion, seeking to devour the faith of the child of God.

There are five lessons or themes of the book of Daniel: (1) God is all-knowing; (2) God rules over human affairs; (3) Evil will ultimately be overcome; (4) We have confidence in God because no one can defy Him; and (5) God is still on the throne. The administrators, governors, counselors, and captains were planning a conspiracy against Daniel. In the face of danger, Daniel practiced three lessons to help turn his dilemma around. The first lesson was that Daniel did not allow his situation to determine his destiny. King Darius did not know Daniel's God, but Daniel knew the greatness of God's authority. For this reason, Daniel put his trust in the power of God. In Psalm 37, we learn that the Lord will help us and deliver us from the wicked and save us because our trust is in what God is able to do, not what man can do. Daniel's faith was being tested, and despite what it looked like, he put his trust not in the present dilemma but in the power of the Almighty God.

The second lesson was the foundation of his faith. Because Daniel was confident in the power of God, he understood that we serve a mighty God. And he knew God's track record. Lesson 3 was that Daniel kept his trust in God. The Bible says that no wounds or bite marks were found on Daniel's body. However, the men who falsely accused him were bought and thrown into the lion's den, along with their wives and children. As believers, we must walk in the power of God, even when people try to do us wrong. We are responsible to respond with a Christlike attitude. The lion's den was Daniel's means of punishment or death, but God turned his situation around. We must walk in the fruit of the Spirit: self-control. We need to understand that it does not matter how bad the situation might look, it does not matter what your friends think about you, it does not matter what your family thinks about you, it does not matter how bad people might talk about you. God wants you to know that what the devil meant for bad, He can turn it around to work for His glory. We have to understand that God is working in as well as through the situation. Remember the God whom we serve is going to help us come out victorious. God has a tight grip on His children, and He won't let go. Nehemiah in chapter 4 teaches us that when Nehemiah and the people were rebuilding the wall of Jerusalem, sometimes you've got to work with one hand and hold a weapon in the other. What you thought would destroy you, God will use to bring you back to His way of living. The Lord wants to rebuild what the devil has torn down in your life. The Lord wants to turn on what the devil has turned off. The Lord wants to restore what the devil has destroyed in your life. But this turnabout can only happen through your obedience to His Word.

CHAPTER 4

⁓

God Can Still Use You

I shall not die,
but live and declare the works of the Lord.
—Psalm 118:17 (NKJV)

As Christians, sometimes we live our lives claiming to know Jesus but not demonstrating our love for Jesus as we live out our faith. As we grow in our walk with God, our goal as Christians should not change. Our life goals should be centered on Jesus, and our focus should be on advancing God's agenda for our lives. There are times in our Christian journey when we can be very comfortable in our walk with Christ, and we become satisfied with a mediocre walk with Him. We need to get back to the basics, understanding, knowing that without Christ working in our lives, it is impossible to live a spiritually transformed life. Therefore, to be in God's presence and to walk in the power of God are the essences of being a disciple of Jesus Christ. In today's society, many people go to church for entertainment instead of to receive instruction for living. Many pastors have become gospel superstars who are larger than life but do not walk in the true nature of God's power. Many Christians have fallen into the trap of living as counterfeit believers. Matthew 5:13–16 (NKJV) says, "We are the salt of the earth: but if the salt have lost his flavor, wherewith shall it be salted? it is thenceforth good for nothing, but to be cast out, and to be trodden under foot of men. We are the light of the world. A city that is set on a hill cannot be hid. Neither do men light a candle, and put it under a bushel, but on a candlestick; nor does it give light unto all that are in the house. Let your light so shine before men, that they may see your good works, and glorify your Father which is in heaven." We are not being the salt that God created us to be. We have lost our flavor, and we worship God as a routine instead of as giving honor to Him. Our revivals are nothing more than emotionally addictive experiences. Jesus said in Matthew 12:25 (NKJV), "Every kingdom divided against itself will be ruined, and every city, nation or household divided against itself will not stand." We must understand that God created the standard that we should live by, and Jesus is the example.

We also need to understand that there are two lifestyles in the church today. One is characterized by wickedness and error; the second is characterized by God's holiness and truth. The Bible teaches that in the last days, people will be treacherous, conceited, lovers of pleasure rather than lovers of God, having the form of godliness but denying its power. Paul, in his letters to Timothy, instructed believers to have nothing to do with people who were treacherous, conceited, and lovers of pleasure. From the look of things, many of us have become Christians who have the posture but not the Spiritual power. The church has begun to assimilate with those who are serving with evil intentions. Our churches have become entertainment centers, while people are dying spiritually and combating life's issues that can seem too overwhelming at times. We have become educated but not enlightened; we have college degrees, but we have not been delivered from the addiction of doing what feels good. We have learned how to be denominational, but we are not living with the Holy Spirit working in our lives. That is why the forces of darkness have been able to blind so any of us to the point that we can no longer see with Spiritual vision eyes and understand the truth of God's Word in our hearts. The Bible teaches us in John 20:31 (NKJV), "These are written that you may believe that Jesus is the Christ and that by believing that, you may have life in His Name."

We must understand that God's purpose is to build up believers. God wants us to be able to stand amid trouble and still walk in victory. Our hope is in the glory of God, and we need to rejoice in the middle of our troubles because God often uses trouble to develop us in a place where we can hear His voice. We have the light of Jesus Christ in us, and greater is He who is in us than He who is in the world. The God that we serve wants the body of Christ to understand how to live in the fullness of God's power.

In John 12:27–35 (NKJV), there are three lessons that deal with walking in the power of God:

> *Lesson 1:* God wants to glorify His name through the church. We must understand that there were revelations during the days of Jesus that clearly broke the norm. We must understand that the body of Christ is growing weary because of church folks taking what belongs to God and playing with it. God wants to be glorified by His believers. Jesus said in John 10:27 (NKJV), "My sheep listen to my voice; I know them and they follow me." We have to know that He is our great shepherd. He is the mighty King and the Master of our lives. Today we are not resting in the power of God's authority. The church as we know it has become a den of thieves, and we are not using the things that God has given us to bring Him maximum glory. The prophet Joel said, "In the Last days God would pour out his spirit on all flesh, our sons and daughters would prophecy. Our young men would dream dreams and on my servants would pour out my spirit in those days and they will prophesy" (Joel 2:28 NKJV).
>
> We must understand that God's Word never changes. But what does change is the methodology that He uses to meet all our needs. The methods He uses with us change depending on what God needs to be accomplished in your life.
>
> *Lesson 2:* If Jesus is lifted up, He will draw all men unto himself. Understand that the cross was and still is the supreme exaltation of God's glory. We have to understand that Jesus Christ is the mechanism that draws us into the saving power of God's grace. Jesus is the only one who brings unity to the entire Christian faith, regardless of our nationalities, ethnic affiliations, or social statuses. We must be reminded that Jesus needs to be lifted up over the

pastor, over church leaders, and over church committee members. We must clothe our minds with righteousness and do things in a way that God would be glorified. The natural must put on the spiritual, and the temporary must put on the everlasting. We need to understand that as Christians, it is mandatory for us to be obedient to the Bible's instructions because it will guide us to spiritual growth and development.

Lesson 3: Walk in the light, and be committed to the truth. Understand that Jesus is the light of the world. John 1:4–5 (NKJV) teaches us that in Jesus Christ was life, and life was the light of men, and the light shined in darkness, and the darkness comprehended it not. John 8:12 (NKJV) teaches us that Jesus is the light of the world, and whosoever follows Him will never walk in darkness but have the light of life within. God called us to a greater walk as well as a greater commitment because He has called us to do great things for Him. Remember, God's greatness is evident in what He creates. Jacob called Him Jehovah Rohi, the Mighty God. Ezekiel called Him Jehovah Shammah, the Lord is there. Isaac told Jacob that He is El Shaddai, the God who is all-sufficient. And Gideon called him Jehovah Shalom. So come out of the darkness, and walk in the victory that only the Lord our God can provides for us.

CHAPTER 5

────── ⟨✦⟩ ──────

God's Nature Is in You

And Jesus looking upon them saith,
with men it is impossible,
but not with God: for with God all things are possible.
—Mark 10:27 (KJV)

There is a connection between Adam and Christ but yet a very unique difference. Adam in the Old Testament introduced sin and death into the world, while Jesus Christ in the New Testament brought righteousness and eternal life. Adam stands for man's condemnation, and Jesus stands for the believer's justification. As the body of Christ, we need to understand that our hope is not to be equated with unfound optimism. On the contrary, it is the blessed assurance of our future in Jesus that is revealed to us in the death of Christ. We just don't want to come to church and be moved by the Spirit of God through worship; we want to live by the Spirit of God. Many of us go to church Sunday after Sunday, searching for the things of God, but never living the new covenant life that comes through believing in the Lord Jesus Christ. The church has failed to guide and equip the people of God to live up to the standard for Christian living according to the Word of the God. The Bible teaches us that from the disobedience of one man, many were made sinners through Adam. So through the obedience of another man, many were made to be righteous through Jesus. So the Law of the Old Testament made sin even more sinful by revealing to us what sin is in contrast to God's holiness. Where sin increases, grace should increase all the more. So sanctification is not a mere religious practice but a standard that Christians are expected to live by because of Christ's blood being shed on the cross.

Paul wrote in his second letter in 2 Timothy about counterfeit Christians, who had a form of godliness but were not walking in the power of the Holy Spirit. I am talking about the middle-of-the-road believers who pretended to have a holiness they really did not live by. Sanctification is not merely an external covering; it is a sap in a root that is interwoven within. We should live our lives separated from the world's way of doing things. We have to remember that true holiness is an inner process that comes from God's nature.

We are sanctified by: (1) the Spirit, (2) the Word of God, and (3) our faith. The reference to the standards of sanctification is in the example of Jesus Christ. In this process of God sanctifying us, He does not want to change our characters; He wants to develop us through regeneration to be just like Jesus. The Bible says that there is no salvation in any other name but in the name of Jesus. We can never forget that only the power of God can help us to live sanctified. You might have tried to live sanctified through your own power and failed because in order to live a life that is holy, we must put our trust in the Jesus Christ.

The apostle Paul explains how God has provided for our redemption and justification in Romans 6:1–14 (KJV):

> What shall we say then? Shall we continue in sin, that grace may abound? God forbid. How shall we, that are dead to sin, live any longer therein? Know ye not, that so many of us as were baptized into Jesus Christ were baptized into his death? Therefore we are buried with him by baptism into death: that like as Christ was raised up from the dead by the glory of the Father, even so we also should walk in newness of life. For if we have been planted together in the likeness of his death, we shall be also in the likeness of his resurrection; Knowing this, that our old man is crucified with him, that the body of sin might be destroyed, that henceforth we should not serve sin. For he that is dead is freed from sin. Now if we

be dead with Christ, we believe that we shall also live with him; knowing that Christ being raised from the dead dies no more; death hath no more dominion over him. For in that he died, he died unto sin once: but in that he lives, he lives unto God. Likewise reckon you also yourselves to be dead indeed unto sin, but alive unto God through Jesus Christ our Lord. Let not sin therefore reign in your mortal body, that ye should obey it in the lusts thereof. Neither yields your members as instruments of unrighteousness unto sin: but yield yourselves unto God, as those that are alive from the dead, and your members as instruments of righteousness unto God. For sin shall not have dominion over you: for ye are not under the law, but under grace.

The apostle Paul also teaches us that it is unthinkable to sin upon the blood of Jesus Christ (Romans 6:15–23 KJV):

What then? shall we sin, because we are not under the law, but under grace? God forbid. Know ye not, that to whom ye yield yourselves servants to obey, his servants ye are to whom ye obey; whether of sin unto death, or of obedience unto righteousness? But God be thanked, that ye were the servants of sin, but ye have obeyed from the heart that form of doctrine which was delivered you. Being then made free from sin, you became the servants of righteousness. I speak after the manner of men because of the infirmity of your flesh: for as ye have yielded your members servants to uncleanness and to iniquity unto iniquity; even so now yield your members servants to righteousness unto holiness. For when ye were the servants of sin, ye were free from righteousness. What fruit had ye then in those things whereof ye are now ashamed? For the end of those things is death. But now being made free from sin, and become servants to God, ye have your fruit unto holiness, and the end everlasting life. For the wages of sin is death; but the gift of God is eternal life through Jesus Christ our Lord.

Paul writes to the Christians in Rome that we have freedom from sin through salvation for three major reasons:

1. Freedom from sin's tyranny
2. Freedom from the law's condemnation
3. Life in the power of the Holy Spirit

The lessons that he taught then are just as relevant now. Paul dealt with our union with Christ Jesus, that we are saved by His blood, and we have experience with Jesus through His death, burial, and resurrection. A record has been left for us so that we will understand that we have died and been raised with Jesus through experiential knowledge. We should also understand that we are God's children through adoption. What that means is we have victory over sin through Jesus Christ, and we are no longer in bondage to sin. The problem is that many of us are still living with Adam in the driver's seat. The truth is many of us really want God's blessings, but we don't want to let go of our addictions to the sinful nature. I have come to discover that the church and the nightclub share a commonality, and that is people come looking to find something that will satisfy the void in their lives. Most people are looking for consistent truth. We must understand that theirs is a force that places us in bondage to our sin nature.

But there is a greater force that wants to give us life. We used to be dominated by the sin nature in our lives, but once we became born again through the blood of Jesus Christ, we came into a new way of walking and a new way of thinking. He who is in Christ is a new creature; old things are passed away, and all things are made new. My old self has been rendered powerless according to Roman 6:16–18 (KJV): "Know not, that to whom ye yield yourselves servants to obey, his servants ye are to whom ye obey; whether of sin unto death, or of obedience unto righteousness? But God be thanked, that ye were the servants of sin, but ye have obeyed from the heart that form of doctrine which was delivered you. Being then made free from sin, ye became the servants of righteousness."

We have been set free from the bondage of sin nature. We have changed masters, and our minds are now focused on being pleasing to our heavenly Father.

CHAPTER 6

Performing Under Pressure

Have Faith in God. For verily I say
unto you, that whosoever
shall say unto this mountain, be removed
and be thou cast into the sea; and shall not
doubt in his heart, but shall believe that those
things which he saith shall come to pass;
he shall have whatsoever he saith.
Therefore I say unto you,
what things so ever you desire, when you pray, believe that
you receive them, and you shall have them.
—Mark 11:22–24 (KJV)

The pressure we feel can cause us to doubt our positions in Christ. Your life should demonstrate the full expression of God's forgiveness and blessings that should flow through your faith in God. Your position in Christ has moved you from death to life because your life should now be under the control of Jesus Christ. We must set our minds on things above, not on earthly things, because your old self is dead. Your life is now hidden with Christ. Jesus is your life now; He is the One you should identify with, not the pressures you face in life. The real nature of pressure comes from our inabilities to control the outcomes of any situations in our lives. Peer pressure can come from our cultural experiences, and it has no age requirement. We begin having our societyies' cultures instilled in us from infancy onward, first of all by the family into which we are born or adopted. This process of acculturation continues as we are exposed to our environments, schooling, religious education, and friends or peers because many of those "bad" behaviors aren't seen as "bad" anymore. Many of today's pressures are felt not as verbal invitations and temptations but as unspoken expectations. What are we pressured to do?

> Pressure 1—To have the perfect body
> Pressure 2—To be dressed and groomed properly
> Pressure 3—To be socially excepted
> Pressure 4—To drink and use drugs
> Pressure 5—To be materialistic
> Pressure 6—To have premarital sex

Because we are followers of Christ, our rebellious natures should no longer rule us. Our new realities should confirm, not contradict our relationship with Christ. There are two results of overwhelming pressure.

> Result 1—Pressure can force you into moral dilemmas.
> Result 2—Pressure can lead you into believing and buying into the devil's lies.

Because of the pressures of life, it is possible as a Christian to say you love Jesus and your life still be wrapped up in selfishness, stubbornness, pride, and arrogance. I would like to share some strategies for dealing with negative pressure.

> Strategy 1—Realize that life's pressure is a spiritual battle that young people will fight constantly.
> Strategy 2—Pray, pray, pray.
> Strategy 3—Model the Christian lifestyle.
> Strategy 4—Help young people develop a God-centered self-image.
> Strategy 5—Get involved in positive Christian fellowship groups.

Strategy 6—Understand that Christians influence other Christians, for better or for worse.

As part of our experiences with Christ, the apostle Paul emphasizes ten things that should be evident in our behaviors and help us to perform under pressure. In Ephesians 4, Paul lists the behavioral flaws that can potentially discredit your walk with God:

1. Do not try to be something that you are not.
2. Tell the truth.
3. Do not let your anger control you.
4. Do not yield to the devil's bullying tactics.
5. Do not steal from anyone.
6. Share with those who are in need.
7. Do not say things that will tear others down.
8. Do not disgrace God by the way you live.
9. Get rid of all bitterness—rage/anger, brawling/slander, every form of malice.
10. Be kind and compassionate to each other.

These ten things should be demonstrated in every Christians' attitudes and behaviors because you have experienced the love of God, which is in Christ. As Christians, we should be moving in a new nature, heading in a new direction, and living in a new way.

CHAPTER 7

———— ✍ ————

Hold on, and Don't Let Go

> Then Jesus said to the centurion, Go your way
> and as you have believed, so let it be
> done for you; and his servant
> was healed that same hour.
> —Matthew 8:13 (NKJV)

God is calling us to place total confidence in Him because He has purposed our lives. God has ordered every outcome to the very minute detail. Through the confidence that we have in the power of our salvation, we are to focus our way of life to being faithful to God's Word. The faithfulness that they learn about through scripture is not a blind unintelligent act of the mind or the will of man. On the contrary, it is and rests upon having the knowledge of God as He reveals Himself through His Word. Faith through knowledge leads to commitment. In the lives of many Old Testament saints, faith was the root that compelled them to be thankful and to trust and believe in the promises of God. There are two persons to whom all things are possible: Jesus Christ and the believer. In these two positions there is no room for doubt or fear. When we doubt what God is able to do, we condemn ourselves; anything that is not produced out of our spiritual relationships through Christ is done out of our sin nature. When we are faced with challenges in life, we often allow faith to turn into fear because our focus is not on how God has kept us in the past.

We give most of our attention on our situations, not the God who rules over all situations. Standing on the faithfulness of God understands that God is in all, and He moves without restrictions or limitations. Faith accepts what reason cannot understand because it is our reason that looks at the problem. But it is our faith that sees God promise amid the problem. It is the reasoning of our minds that see obstacles, but it is our faith that overcomes our fears and doubts. It is our reason that holds on to the past, but it is our faith that gives us hope for tomorrow. This is why in chapter 39 of Isaiah, the prophet Isaiah urged Hezekiah to not use logic but to cast himself on the Lord for protection. We should always remember that God will always be true to His Word. In the fortieth chapter of Isaiah, God sends comfort for His people, and in this comfort from God we grow to understand how God is able to deliver and restore people who are in distressed situations. If we trust in God's perfect will while we are waiting on Him, we will be able to draw our strength from the One who gives strength to those who have no strength and power to those who have no power. We must learn to cast all our anxieties on Him because He really does cares for us. God wants us to be focused on His will for our lives; He wants us to use His power to accomplish great things for the kingdom of God. God is looking for people who will trust Him when it looks like there is no way out. The Bible says in Galatians 6:9 (KJV), "Let us not grow weary in well doing for in due seasons, we shall reap if we faint not."

God does not want us to draw back; he wants us to move forward. We need to understand that there is power in waiting on the Lord. We should remember that while we are waiting, it is imperative that we remain grateful. Why? Because God wants to help build our faith, and the more faith we demonstrate, the more strength we receive to be patient and wait on the blessing from God. The Bible teaches us that faith is the only thing that pleases God.

CHAPTER 8

❧

Change Is Good

And this is the confidence that we have
in Him, that if we ask anything
according to His will, He hearth us; and if we know
that He hear us, whatsoever we ask, we know that we have
the petitions that we desire of Him.

—1 John 5:14–15 (KJV)

There are times when we feel that the Lord is not as personal as the Bible says He is. There are times we believe that the Lord has better things to do than to help us in our situations. The truth is as Christians, there are times when we feel we have failed God because we have not been patient in a life situation, when we should have trusted God more, or we took things into our own hands instead of trusting in God. Because of these challenges, we approach Jesus as if we have everything together and know all the answers. We start to treat our Christian relationships with Jesus Christ like our personal people relationships and begin to muddy up the two. If we are going to move to a stronger spiritual level in Christ, we are going to have to approach the area of change in a more committed way. If we are going to do great things in the body of Christ and bring forth much fruit, we have to choose to walk by faith and allow Jesus Christ, who is the sustainer of life, to have total control over our lives.

In Luke chapter 7, we read the account of a sinful woman who approached

Jesus, even though the people thought that it was improper for her to do so. They wondered, *What could this sinful person need from the Messiah?* But this sinful women approached Jesus with an earnest dilemma. She must have heard about Jesus, and out of repentance, she was determined to lead a new life. This woman was in need of something that was divine, that only Christ could do for her. This woman came out because she was expecting a change to come over her life that would help her move through her difficulties. She was in need of what Jesus had to offer that would give her power to live out her life walking in His forgiveness. Jesus did not care what she had done. She sat at His feet because she needed to be washed and forgiven so that she could walk in her God-given purpose.

In 2 Corinthians chapter 1, we are reminded that it is God who established and anointed us to operate in our God-given spiritual gifts. So it is God's anointing that gives us purpose, stability, peace, and hope in Christ. It is that same anointing that protects us from danger and gives us power over sin in our lives. Jesus knew that this woman may have been proud, but when Jesus looked at this women, He saw someone who needed to be saved.

> And behold, a woman in the city who was a sinner, when she knew that Jesus sat at the table in the Pharisee's house, brought an alabaster flask of fragrant oil, and stood at His feet behind Him weeping; and she began to wash His feet with her tears, and wiped them with the hair of her head; and she kissed His feet and anointed them with the fragrant oil. Now when the Pharisee who had invited Him saw this, he spoke to himself, saying, "This Man, if He were a prophet, would know who and what manner of woman this is who is touching Him, for she is a sinner." And Jesus answered and said to him, "Simon, I have something to say to you." So he said, "Teacher, say it." "There was a certain creditor who had two debtors. One owed five hundred denarii, and the other fifty. And when they had nothing with which to repay, he freely forgave them both. Tell Me, therefore, which of them will love him more?" Simon answered and said, "I suppose the one whom he forgave more." And He said to him, "You have rightly judged." Then He turned to

the woman and said to Simon, "Do you see this woman? I entered your house; you gave Me no water for My feet, but she has washed My feet with her tears and wiped them with the hair of her head. You gave Me no kiss, but this woman has not ceased to kiss My feet since the time I came in. You did not anoint My head with oil, but this woman has anointed My feet with fragrant oil. Therefore I say to you, her sins, which are many, are forgiven, for she loved much. But to whom little is forgiven, the same loves little." Then He said to her, "Your sins are forgiven." And those who sat at the table with Him began to say to themselves, "Who is this who even forgives sins?" Then He said to the woman, "Your faith has saved you. Go in peace." (Luke 7:36–50 NKJV)

This woman did not care who was watching her or talking about her. She didn't care who looked at her in a strange way. I believe that she didn't care what people might have thought about her. We have to understand that our relationships with Jesus Christ are more important than the condition that we might find ourselves in. God never changes, but He promotes change to take place in our lives every day. Our lives as Christians are and will always be a continuation of ordained changes to shape us into mature believers.

CHAPTER 9

─── ❧ ───

Don't Let Go

Let the weak say I am strong.
—Joel 3:10 (NKJV)

As I was growing up, I used to go up the street to talk with a pastor who lived in my neighborhood. At that time in my life there were some very difficult things going on, and I needed some godly advice. This pastor's words of encouragement were always on target and helped me to hold to God's unchanging hand. As Christians, whether we want to admit it or not, we sometimes have a difficult time holding on when life situations feel a little overwhelming. That is one of the reasons I believe many of us live in a defeated mindset in which we feel helpless and hopeless. As we fall victim to our personal conflicts or life situations, we cannot stop believing that God moves beyond our problems and our understanding. We need to know that God works like a master craftsman, weaving His will in and out of our lives so that His perfect will can be done. Therefore, we should walk in victory over our not so good situations and circumstance. Holding onto the strength that works through our trust in God's purpose in what we experience allows God to accomplish His perfected purpose in our lives. We should always remember that God wants us to walk in the authority of His Word, which moves beyond all our disappointments, beyond all our heartaches, beyond all our problems, beyond all our pains, and beyond all our discomforts.

As we continue to trust in God's sovereign rule over us, we have to remember in all of our decision-making that God is right, and He is faithful in caring for us and working out His purpose in our lives. The Bible teaches us in 2 Timothy 2:13 (NKJV), "If we are faithful, he will remain faithful, for he cannot disown himself." So it is our faith in God through Jesus Christ that helps us to hold on in difficult times. As Christians, we should understand that faith is the power of God manifested in the life of the believer who puts absolute trust in God's promises. With this faith, we are able to be pleasing to God. But without faith, we cannot please Him. It is faith that helps us to overcome all the impossibilities in life. We must be reminded that it is our faith in God through salvation that teaches us how to follow God. And it is by our faith that we are connected to the power of God. In Psalm 30, David faced a very challenging dilemma, and through his struggles, God wanted him to know that the power of the Lord will give us strength to overcome any obstacles. If only we would prepare our hearts to obey God's instructions, stretch out our hands toward the heavens, submit our ways to the Lord, and trust Him to show up with all power. The Bible teaches us that God is not a man that he should lie. Keep in mind that whatever God has promised to do in our lives He will do. Even if you have to bear your cross alone, hold on to the God who is the same yesterday, today, and in your future. The apostle Paul wrote in Romans chapter 6 that we were buried with Jesus through baptism into death, and that gives us our credentials for spiritual authority. Just as Jesus Christ was raised from the dead by the glory of the Father, because of this Christian reality, we should live to glorify God the Father through daily demonstration. So when it looks like it is your darkest hour, God is about to bring morning back into your life. As Jesus said in Matthew 17:20 (NKJV), "that if you have the faith of a mustard seed, you can move mountains."

CHAPTER 10

―❧―

In Need of a Real Relationship

Who His own self bare our sins in
His own body on the tree,
that we being dead to sins, should live unto righteousness;
by whose stripes you were healed.

—1 Peter 2:24 (KJV)

When people talk about things that they like or dislike, we generally want them to tell us the truth. Though we want to be told the truth, we sometimes can't handle the truth about most situations. Truth exposes us and can cause us to move into a state of denial, thinking that the whole world is against us. The Bible teaches us that the truth shall make us free.

Truth can only be defined in our example of what Christ demonstrated on the cross, which gave you and I access to a divine relationship. My friend, Jesus is the way, the truth, and the life. But our understanding of what truth is can be clouded by the lust of our flesh. As Christians, we can get so focused on an outward expression of religion and our human efforts. We base many of our relationships with people on premises of how well we know them or what we can gain from them. The more we come to know a person, the more we can identify with their strengths and weaknesses. But when it comes to Christian relationships, we tend to stray from the spiritual truth because we don't want to be exposed by God. The Bible teaches us that God is sovereign, and He uses everything in our lives to keep us growing in this loving relationship. We cannot forget that God will always hold us accountable to obey Him as we live in His powerful presence. This is why we gravitate to the hardship of natural things instead of walking in God's promise through spiritual things. The more we get to know Christ through our spiritual relationships, the more we see how great God is and how weak and sinful we are.

There were times in the Bible when people strayed from what was God's will for them. We learn about this kind of willful disobedience through Israel, God's chosen people in the Old Testament. The practice of spiritual truth leads us and guides us into the things of God, which help us trust in the instructions that the Bible teaches and that we should believe and follow. The apostle Paul's writings paint a very clear picture of how Christians can have a limited relationship with God and don't even know it. In Matthew 26:30–31 (NKJV), Jesus told the disciples their relationships with Him would come with a cost, Jesus said,

> For this is my blood of the new testament, which is shed for many for the remission of sins. But I say unto you, I will not drink henceforth of this fruit of the vine, until that day when I drink it new with you in my Father's kingdom. And when they had sung an hymn, they went out into the mount of Olives. Then Jesus said unto them, All ye shall be offended because of me this night: for it is written, I will smite the shepherd, and the sheep of the flock shall be scattered abroad. But after I am raised again, I will go before you into Galilee.

Zechariah chapter 13 points to the evidence of what that relationship cost Christ: "strike the Shepard, and the sheep will be scattered." This was prophecy from the Old Testament that would be fulfilled in the gospel message of the New Testament. The relationship barrier was destroyed in the New Testament because Jesus was a man who fulfilled God's promise by the shedding of His blood on Calvary. What happened three days after the death and burial of Christ was the salvation, the saving grace for generations to come. After Jesus was arrested, Peter one of Jesus's disciples, became the poster child of what this limited relationship looked like. Peter was committed to the mission of Christ before the cross, but once the religious leaders handcuffed Christ and He was headed to the cross to be crucified, Peter denied Jesus, therefore compromising his commitment to Christ. Peter was always messing up and doing things without putting his relationship with Christ in the forefront. Because of our personal fears, we often do just what Peter did. We reject our commitments with Jesus and compromise our belief systems because we don't want people to know that we really do love Jesus. We push our relationships with Christ aside to please people. We must come to understand that if it had not been for the Lord on our side, where would we be today? Peter loved Jesus and adored Him, but it was out of Peter's arrogance that he would tell Jesus that he would never leave or deny Him: "And the Lord said, Simon, Simon, behold, Satan hath desired to have you, that he may sift you as wheat: But I have prayed for thee, that thy faith fail not: and when thou art converted, strengthen thy brethren. And he said unto him, Lord, I am ready to go with thee, both into prison, and to death.' Jesus says, 'Simon Peter, Satan desires to sift you like wheat. But I have prayed for you, that your faith may not fail'" (Luke 22:31–33 KJV).

The devil is fierce and cruel, and he wants to take us out. But Jesus never stopped loving, and God has never stopped loving you. God wants to use you to serve Him and help you become an example to others who might be struggling with the same things you have struggled with. Peter should remind you of how easy it is to fall into the same trap of disconnection that happened to Peter. When he was consumed and sifted by the devil as he denied Jesus, he placed himself in a relationship that went from being liberating to desolation. You can never forget that God knows who we are and what His will is for each of us. That is why Jesus looked past what Peter said and told Peter the truth about himself. Remember, Peter was the disciple who had walked on water. He had also seen Jesus transform on the mountain of transfiguration. Peter lost focus and was misdirected by his fear.

We should live in God's power and focus on pleasing the Almighty God. We learn in 1 Thessalonians 4:1 (NKJV) how we should live as Christians: "Finally brothers, we instruct you to live in order to please God." You cannot live to please your friends, your boss, your supervisor, your peers, or your family. It is life's responsibility as Christians to honor and please God in everything we do. It's simple: We are here to please God. "He will equip us with everything good for doing his will" (Hebrews 13:21 NKJV). So in other words, God will work in us what is pleasing to Him through Jesus Christ. It is not wise for you to underestimate God and what He can do when you put your trust in Him. Proverbs 9:2 (NKJV) teaches us that "If you are wise, your wisdom will reward you: If you are a mocker, you alone will suffer."

Many of us are suffering and struggling today because we are trying to fool God, and in the process, we are deceiving ourselves. We must repent for the wrongdoings and continue to hold on to God's unchanging commitment and love toward us. When God commanded Jonah to leave his native city in Israel to go to Nineveh and preach, Jonah was furious. Jonah asked, "Why should God care about those pagans?" Jonah deliberately took a ship headed in the opposite direction, which was defiant disobedience. A great storm arose, and Jonah accepted responsibility for the danger, requesting that he be thrown overboard. A great fish swallowed him, and after three days, he was disgorged onto the land. Chastened, Jonah then went to Nineveh to preach. When the people of Nineveh repented, Jonah was resentful. He sulked outside the city. God then taught him a very valuable lesson about obedience. Let us trust in the Master's plan for your lives.

CHAPTER 11

―⁓―

Understanding Yourself

And it shall come to pass, if thou
shalt hearken diligently unto
the voice of the Lord thy God, to observe
and to do all His commandments.
All these blessings shall come on you, and overtake you, if
you shall hearken to the voice of the Lord your God.
—Deuteronomy 28:1–2 (KJV)

Jesus connected the kingdom of God to a spiritual reality or realm where the will of God is recognized as being supreme and where God exercises His sovereign right to rule over all situations. You must understand that knowing who you are in Christ will help you live a spirit-filled life with a kingdom mind and attitude. This is the kind of mind that is focused on doing what will bring glory to God. A kingdom way of thinking can help you operate above our physical needs. The carnal mind ignores God's faithfulness. God will provide. The kingdom mind knows who is always in control of the outcome. Luke 12:25–28 (NKJV) tell us, "And which of you by worrying can add one cubit to his stature? If you then are not able to do the least, why are you anxious for the rest? Consider the lilies, how they grow: they neither toil nor spin; and yet I say to you, even Solomon in all his glory was not arrayed like one of these. If then God so clothes the grass, which today is in the field and tomorrow is thrown into the oven, how much more will He clothe you, O you of little faith?"

The carnal mind ignores God's predetermined Plan. We worry as if God is not in control. The kingdom mind is the antidote for anxiety: "And do not seek what you should eat or what you should drink, nor have an anxious mind. For all these things the nations of the world seek after, and your Father knows that you need these things. But seek the kingdom of God, and all these things shall be added to you" (Luke 12:29–31 NKJV). The carnal mind ignores God's provisions. We have to remember that the God who gives life is also the God who will take care of you. Jesus taught that the kingdom is "at hand" (Matthew 4:17 NKJV).

Jesus's teachings expanded the concept of the spiritual nature of humankind as a part of the spiritual existence of the Creator God. Realization of this through faith brings one within the realm of a spiritual kingdom referred to as the "kingdom of God." To enter the kingdom is the most important thing a person can do. We should be willing to lose all that we have to obtain it—even our lives if need be—because nothing can compare with knowing God now and eternally. We must understand that we are influenced and affected by four areas of development:

1. Socially—We want to fit in with the crowd.
2. Emotionally—We want to be well liked.
3. Physically—We want to look good.
4. Spiritually—For some, this is the least of their concerns.

It is important for us to live a life knowing the answers about who we are through our relationship with Christ. Your identity is now hidden in Jesus Christ.

CHAPTER 12

⌇

Be Driven by the Gift of Love

Oh, give thanks to the Lord, for he is
good! For His mercy endures
forever. Let the redeemed of the Lord say so, whom
He has redeemed from the hand of the enemy.
—Psalm 107:1–2 (NKJV)

As Christians, we need to be aware of the gifts that God has given each of us. We must be very diligent in doing the things that God has called us to do. We must remember that only the things that we do for Jesus Christ will have any eternal relevance. As we take a look at our walk with God in this new millennium, I believe that many of us who say we love Jesus are more focused on developing religious routines instead of sincere relationship. James 1:26–27 (NKJV) says, "If anyone among you thinks he is religious, and does not bridle his tongue but deceives his own heart, this one's religion is useless. Pure and undefiled religion before God and the Father is this: to visit orphans and widows in their trouble, and to keep oneself unspotted from the world." This teaches us that it is our responsibility to help those who are in great need, and religion that God accepts as pure is ministry that looks after orphans and widows in distress.

What is it that we need to do to accomplish the task that God has given you and I? We must represent God's kingdom by sharing our Spiritual gifts with each other in love through serving God. We need more Christians to serve God and be committed to the call of the gospel. I believe that if we are going to become all that we should be as members of Christ's body, we are going to have to give God's love to those in need, share God's love with the world, and spread God's love to those who are bound by sin and trouble in their lives. The apostle Paul, in the first epistle to the church of Corinth in chapter 12, expressed the need to exercise our God-given gifts to fulfill the mission of the church to impact spiritual change in people. Paul wanted to instruct the people to walk in obedience to God's will and emphasized two very important areas of commitment:

1. The different gifts that were given by God for His people to function in the church
2. The necessity of exercising these gifts in love so that the church would be healthy

Paul identifies that even our most spectacular manifestations of God's gifts will mean nothing unless they are motivated by a sincere love for God. As Christians, we have different gifts, and no one gift should be seen as greater than another because all spiritual gifts are given by God for His glory. Paul writes in the twelfth chapter of 1 Corinthians that we are to operate in the best gifts, and that is demonstrated through love. When it came to exercising spiritual gifts through the love of God, Paul understood that

> Love can turn your heartache into hope.
> Love can turn pain into power.
> Love can turn your problems and pressures into promises.
> Love can turn your disappointments into deliverance.
> Love can turn your chaos into clarity.
> Love can turn jealousy into joy.

The apostle Paul wrote in many of his letters about the type of love that God wants us to walk in because everyone who loves has been born of God, and whoever does not love does not know God because God is love. It is the Christian's responsibility to not just love with words but to love with actions. Love is the means by which spiritual gifts are made effective. We must understand that the problems we face today are the same problems the church in Corinth had in the New Testament. The church in Corinth was seeking status because of the use of their gifts, which made them feel good about what they were doing, but God was not the focus of their service. Many of today's Christians behave in the same gestures of the church in Corinth. Today we see more and more people focusing on social status and personal prominence in the church rather than God's promise of love. The Bible teaches us to love because God first loved, and therefore, whenever we love, we are expressing the very nature of God, and it is important that the application of God's love work through our spiritual gifts. We have to understand that we can have faith that can move mountains, but if we don't exercise that faith in love, our efforts to use what God has given us to build up each other in Christ is covered in selfishness and is not Christ-centered. Even if you give all your stuff away and surrender your body to be burned for the sake of others, if it is not motivated by love and the use of your spiritual gifts, you will accomplish nothing.

Paul, in many of his letters to the churches that he started, insists one basic principle that must be a focus of your faith: We must be contributors to the building up and the edification of other believers. God is love, and He has given gifts to those who believe to bring glory to God through applied love toward each other. After the pain of broken relationships end, after the anxieties of life slow down and the hurts of your past come to a stop, the love of God will still be with you to help you grow through life challenges. The love of God and your God-given gifts will establish in you and I the power to love your enemies, power to rejoice in truth, power to bear all things in Jesus's name, the power to believe all things according to His Word, and will help us to endure hardships as a good soldiers. The Bible says in 1 Corinthians 13:13 (NKJV), "And now abide Faith, Hope, and Love these three, but the greatest of these is Love." We have to come to a point that the love of Christ should be the focus of our attitudes, behaviors, and conduct as Christian. Let love be your motivation to live in God's healing environment.

CHAPTER 13

─────────────── ❧ ───────────────

Don't Doubt What God Can Do

"My grace is sufficient for you, for My strength is made
perfect in weakness." Therefore most gladly I will
rather boast in my infirmities, that the power of
Christ may rest upon me."
—2 Corinthians 12:9 (NKJV)

In the days that we are living in, it can seem so difficult to get up every morning in the middle of what looks and feels like a desert/wilderness. But amid this pandemic, as believers we must not allow the challenge of what we are facing to tempt us to disconnect from God and each other. God doesn't send deserts in our lives to destroy us. He uses them to develop us to become spirit-filled, more creative, and more effective for His work of ministry. In Luke chapter 4, Jesus was led into the wilderness by the Holy Spirit and tempted by the devil for forty days and nights in the desert. This shows us that Jesus walked in Spiritual power as the righteous Son of God. It also teaches us the importance of trusting in and following God's wisdom in every situation face in life. We should always remind ourselves as believers that life is never going to be easy, but in the name of Jesus, we have the victory. We have to hold on to the truth of the Bible that encourages us to trust that whenever God presses someone, it is to define who we are in Him. It shows us what He has created in us as His church and to be witnesses for His glory. The apostle Paul reminds us in 2 Corinthians chapter 4 that we have this treasure in earthen vessels that the excellence of the power may be of God and not of us. We are hard-pressed on every side yet not crushed; we are perplexed but not in despair, persecuted but not forsaken, struck down but not destroyed. We are always carrying around, as the body of Christ, the dying of the Lord Jesus, so the life of Jesus may be manifested in our bodies to live for His glory and to do His will. Jesus had to endure the wilderness experience because it would position Him for the road to Calvary and then His resurrection. We must remind ourselves that we are the church of the living God and understand that even in the middle of a crisis, God has a plan for His church. Even in a pandemic, we still have to walk in His power and stay committed to His plan to continue to follow His Great Commission.

Jesus reminds us in Matthew chapter 28 that He has given the church His authority to seek and save the lost. He tells us to go and make disciples of all nations, baptizing them in the name of the Father and of the Son and of the Holy Spirit, teaching them to observe all that He has commanded us. In times of uncertainty, we must have firm belief in that blessed assurance that Jesus is mine, and He is in control. We have to keep fighting the good fight in faith and never doubt God's power to heal, to provide, and to save the lost in this temporary new normal.

NOTES

If your church or organization is interested in having Pastor Edward D. Harris Sr. come to share, *God's Healing Environment* at your next service or event, he can be connected at,

Pastor Edward D. Harris Sr.
Christ Power Church & Ministries
4545 Harford Road
Baltimore, Maryland 21214
E-mail: worship@christpower.org
Church website: christpowerchurchbaltimore.org

Printed in the United States
By Bookmasters